W9-CXY-585

THE PASSIONATE LIFE

BIBLE STUDY SERIES

John
ETERNAL LOVE

12-WEEK STUDY GUIDE

BroadStreet
PUBLISHING

Broadstreet Publishing Group, LLC
Racine, Wisconsin, USA
BroadStreetPublishing.com

The Passionate Life Bible Study Series
JOHN: ETERNAL LOVE

© 2016 Broadstreet Publishing Group

Edited by Jeremy Bouma

ISBN-13: 978-1-4245-5162-0 (softcover)
ISBN-13: 978-1-4245-5250-4 (e-book)

All rights reserved. No part of this book may be reproduced in any form, except for brief quotations in printed reviews, without permission in writing from the publisher.

All Bible text is from The Passion Translation®, including the following books: *Matthew: Our Loving King, John: Eternal Love, The Psalms: Poetry on Fire*, and *Hebrews and James: Faith Works*. Cpyright © 2014, 2015. Used by permission of The Passion Translation and BroadStreet Publishing Group, LLC, Racine, Wisconsin, USA. All rights reserved. www.thePassionTranslation.com

Cover design by Chris Garborg at www.garborgdesign.com
Typesetting by Katherine Lloyd at www.theDESKonline.com

Printed in the United States of America
16 17 18 19 20 5 4 3 2 1

Contents

Using This Passionate Life Bible Study

The psalmist declares, "Truth's shining light guides me in my choices and decisions; the revelation of your Word makes my pathway clear" (Psalm 119:105).

This verse forms the foundation of the Passionate Life Bible Study series. Not only do we want to kindle within you a deep, burning passion for God and his Word, but we also want to let the Word's light blaze a bright path before you to help you make truth-filled choices and decisions, while encountering the heart of God along the way.

God longs to have his Word expressed in a way that would unlock the passion of his heart. Inspired by The Passion Translation but usable with any Bible translation, this is a heart-level Bible study, from the passion of God's heart to the passion of your heart. Our goal is to trigger inside you an overwhelming response to the truth of the Bible.

DISCOVER. EXPLORE. EXPERIENCE. SHARE.

Each of the following lessons is divided into four sections: *Discover the Heart of God*; *Explore the Heart of God*; *Experience the Heart of God*; and *Share the Heart of God*. They are meant to guide your study of the truth of God's Word, while drawing you closer and deeper into his passionate heart for you and your world.

The *Discover* section is designed to help you make observations about the reading. Every lesson opens with the same three questions: What did you notice, perhaps for the first time? What questions do you have? And, what did you learn about the heart of God? There are no right answers here! They are meant to jump-start your journey into God's truth by bringing to the surface your initial impressions about the passage. The other questions help draw your attention to specific points the author wrote and discover the truths God is conveying.

Explore takes you deeper into God's Word by inviting you to think more critically and explain what the passage is saying. Often there is some extra information to highlight and clarify certain aspects of the passage, while inviting you to make connections. Don't worry if the answers aren't immediately apparent. Sometimes you may need to dig a little deeper or take a little more time to think. You'll be grateful you did, because you will have tapped into God's revelation-light in greater measure!

Experience is meant to help you do just that: experience God's heart for you personally. It will help you live out God's Word by applying it to your unique life situation. Each question in this section is designed to bring the Bible into your world in fresh, exciting, and relevant ways. At the end of this section, you will have a better idea of how to make choices and decisions that please God, while walking through life on clear paths bathed in the light of his revelation!

The final section is *Share*. God's Word isn't meant to be merely studied or memorized; it's meant to be shared with other people—both through living and telling. This section helps you understand how the reading relates to growing closer to others, to enriching your fellowship and relationship with your world. It also helps you listen to the stories of those around you, so you can bridge Jesus' story with their stories.

SUGGESTIONS FOR INDIVIDUAL STUDY

Reading and studying the Bible is an exciting journey! It's like reading your favorite novel—where the purpose is encountering the heart and mind of the author through its characters and conflict, plot points, and prose.

This study is designed to help you encounter the heart of God and let his Word to you reach deep down into your very soul—all so you can live and enjoy the life he intends for you. And like with any journey, a number of practices will help you along the way:

1. Begin your lesson time in prayer, asking God to open up his Word to you in new ways, show areas of your heart that need teaching and healing, and correct any area in which you're living contrary to his desires for your life.

2. Read the opening section to gain an understanding of the major themes of the reading and ideas for each lesson.

3. Read through the Scripture passage once, underlining or noting in your Bible anything that stands out to you. Reread the passage again, keeping in mind these three questions: What did you notice, perhaps for the first time? What questions do you have? What did you learn about the heart of God?

4. Write your answers to the questions in this Bible study guide or another notebook. If you do get stuck, first ask God to reveal his Word to you and guide you in his truth. And then, either wait until your small group time or ask your pastor or another respected leader for help.

5. Use the end of the lesson to focus your time of prayer, thanking and praising God for the truth of his Word, for what he has revealed to you, and for how he has impacted your daily life.

SUGGESTIONS FOR SMALL GROUP STUDY

The goal of this study is to understand God's Word for you and your community in greater measure, while encountering his heart along the way. A number of practices will also help your group as you journey together:

1. Group studies usually go better when everyone is prepared to participate. The best way to prepare is to come having read the lesson's Scripture reading beforehand. Following the suggestions in each individual study will enrich your time as a community as well.

2. Before you begin the study, your group should nominate a leader to guide the discussion. While this person should work through the questions beforehand, his or her main job isn't to lecture, but to help move the conversation along by asking the lesson questions and facilitating the discussion.

3. This study is meant to be a community affair where everyone shares. Be sure to listen well, contribute where you feel led, and try not to dominate the conversation.

4. The number one rule for community interaction is: nothing is off-limits! No question is too dumb; no answer is out of bounds. While many questions in this study have "right" answers, most are designed to push you and your friends to explore the passage more deeply and understand what it means for daily living.

5. Finally, be ready for God to reveal himself through the passage being discussed and through the discussion that arises out of the group he's put together. Pray that he would reveal his heart and revelation-light to you all in deeper ways. And be open to being challenged, corrected, and changed.

Again, we pray and trust that this Bible study will kindle in you a burning, passionate desire for God and his heart, while impacting your life for years to come. May it open wide the storehouse of heaven's revelation-light. May it reveal new and greater insights into the mysteries of God and the kingdom-realm life he has for you. And may you encounter the heart of God in more fresh and relevant ways than you ever thought possible!

Introduction to the Gospel of John

Perhaps the most recognizable verse in the Bible is found in John's gospel: "For this is how much God loved the world—he gave his one and only, unique Son as a gift. So now everyone who believes in him will never perish but experience everlasting life" (John 3:16). John's declaration forms the heart of his gospel because it flows from the very heart of God.

While Matthew, Mark, and Luke give us the history of Christ, John writes to unveil the *mystery* of Christ. Jesus is seen as the Lamb of God, the Good Shepherd, the Kind Forgiver, the Tender Healer, the Compassionate Intercessor, and the Great I Am. Who can resist this man when he tugs on your heart to come to him? To read John's gospel is to encounter Jesus. Make this your goal as you read and study his story: encounter the risen Christ in all his glory and love!

We've designed this study to help you discover God's love through John's magnificent biography of history's most fascinating person, Jesus of Nazareth. John said he wrote his gospel "so that you will fully believe that Jesus is the Anointed One, the Son of God, and that through your faith in him you will experience eternal life by the power of his name!" (John 20:31). Embark on an amazing, exciting journey through the Gospel of John to discover the life he has in store for you!

Lesson 1

The Living Expression of God

JOHN 1:1–18

*And so the Living Expression
became a man and lived among us!
And we gazed upon the splendor of his glory,
the glory of the One and Only,
who came from the Father overflowing
with tender mercy and truth!* (John 1:14)

Who is God, and what is he like? Is he angry, ready to hurl lighting bolts down on unsuspecting humans? Is he an unblinking, cosmic stare who can't be bothered by our problems? Today we begin a fascinating journey into this crucial question of faith, discovering a shocking answer from the start: God isn't a distant and removed being but a very present and all-too-loving *Person!* We meet him as the Living Expression.

John has given us this new unique view of God in his gospel, which signifies the presence of God himself in the flesh. Some have translated this rich term as "Word." It could also be translated "Message" or "Blueprint." He's known by another name too: Jesus Christ. Jesus is the eternal Word, the creative Word, and the Word made visible. He is the divine self-expression of all that God is, contains, and reveals in incarnated flesh. God has perfectly expressed himself in Christ.

Do you want to know who God is and what God is like? Get to know Jesus! This study through John's gospel will help you encounter the heart of God through Jesus as the loving God in flesh and blood.

Discover the Heart of God

- After reading John 1:1–18, what did you notice, perhaps for the first time? What questions do you have? What did you learn about the heart of God?

- In 1:1–18, what do we learn about the Living Expression, especially his identity?

- When did the Living Expression come into existence? How does John say the Living Expression was born?

- Why was John the Immerser sent from God? What did he announce about the Living Expression?

- What happened when the "Light of Truth" came into the world?

Explore the Heart of God

- John modeled the opening verses of his gospel after the opening verses in Genesis. Look at Genesis 1:1–5 and compare it to John 1:1–5. What similarities do you notice? How might this be important to John's own message?

- John said the very world God created didn't "recognize [Jesus]," especially his own people. Why should they have? Can you think of any verses and passages from the Hebrew Scriptures that pointed to God coming in the flesh?

- We call 1:13 the *incarnation*, when God became a man by way of a virgin birth. Why is it important that Jesus, the Living Expression, was born of God and not of natural means? Why does it matter that he is fully God, as 1:1 says?

- What does it mean for us that the Living Expression became one of us and lived among us? Why is it significant and why does it matter that Jesus was as much a human as he was God?

- How does Jesus "unfold to us the full explanation of who God truly is" (1:18)?

Experience the Heart of God

- Why do you think it matters to your life that Jesus, the Living Expression, was with, from, and is God? What does it matter for the whole world?

- How does it make you feel knowing that God lived the life you live as Jesus? What does this revelation say about the heart of God?

- John calls the Living Expression, Jesus, "Light." How have you seen this aspect of Christ in your own life?

- What have you discovered about Jesus and the heart of God by following him?

Share the Heart of God

- John said that when the Light of Truth came to the people he created, they did not recognize him. Consider how people in our world have not recognized Jesus, the Living Expression.

- According to 1:12, anyone who takes hold of Jesus' name is "given the authority to become children of God!" Who in your life needs to "take hold" of the name of Jesus? How can you help them?

CONSIDER THIS

Jesus is the eternal Living Expression of God. Literally, God came in flesh and bones! He understands your life because he lived this life. Which means he cares for every ounce of your life. Close by thanking God for becoming one of us in the person of Jesus and showing people who and what he is like.

Lesson 2

The One We've Been Waiting For

JOHN 1:19–2:25

*"We've found him! We've found the One we've been
waiting for! It's Jesus, son of Joseph from Nazareth,
the Anointed One! He's the One that Moses and
the prophets prophesied would come!"* (John 1:45)

Some people spend a lifetime searching for that one person or one thing that will provide fulfillment, offer a place to fit in, and make them whole again. What we discover in this lesson is that Jesus is the One people have been waiting for their whole lives—whether they know it or not!

The first person we meet knew exactly who Jesus was. John the Immerser was commissioned by God to spread far and wide the news that the Mighty One Israel had been waiting for, God's Lamb, had finally arrived to take away the sins of the world. Then several more young men—Andrew, Simon, Philip, and Nathanael—found the one they had been waiting for, too, the Anointed One and Son of God! Jesus confirmed this by his very first miracle when he provided for the practical needs of a wedding in unexpected ways.

What are you longing for? What are you searching for? Continue reading the fascinating story about the God who became one of us, who invites us all to "come follow me."

Discover the Heart of God

- After reading John 1:19–2:25, what did you notice, perhaps for the first time? What questions do you have? What did you learn about the heart of God?

- What did John the Immerser call Jesus when he saw him? Why is this title significant, and how does it give us a glimpse into the heart of God?

- When Andrew found his brother, what did he say he found? What did Philip do when Jesus invited him to "come follow me"? How did Nathanael respond?

- When Jesus walked into the temple, what did he notice? Why did this make him angry? How had it been transformed from what God intended into a "center for merchandise"?

- What reason did John say people were giving for their allegiance to Jesus? Why didn't Jesus entrust himself to the people?

Explore the Heart of God

- What was Isaiah's prophecy concerning the Messiah, and how did John fulfill part of it? See Isaiah 40.

- What picture of God was present at Jesus' baptism in 1:32?

- Why was it so significant that Andrew said to Simon that he had found "the Anointed One"? What did he mean?

- What does it teach us about the heart of God that Jesus' first miracle was turning water into wine?

- At the temple, Jesus said, "After you've destroyed the temple, I will raise it up again in three days" (2:19). What did Jesus mean by this?

Experience the Heart of God

- "What do you want?" (1:38) is a question Jesus asks everyone who seeks to follow him. Do we want something only for ourselves? A ministry? Answers to prayer? Or do we simply want to be with him? How would you answer this question?

- In what ways have you found and experienced what you had been waiting for in relationship with Jesus, just like Philip and Nathanael did?

- How do people in our day react when Christians say Jesus is the One prophesied about, the Anointed One? How have you?

- At the wedding of Cana, Jesus proved himself in a very practical way by providing for Miriam's[1] practical needs. What sort of practical needs do you have? Spend time asking Jesus to do something about them—just as he did for Miriam.

Share the Heart of God

- Two of John's disciples followed after Jesus because they were intrigued and attracted to Jesus, so they wanted to discover more. How can we share the heart of God in a way that creates the same kind of intrigue so that our friends and family want to discover more about Jesus?

---

1 "Miriam" is a literal rendering from the original Greek and Aramaic, which leave the Hebrew as is. She is more widely known as Mary, mother of Jesus.

- How can you practically meet the needs of people in your life like Jesus did at the wedding in Cana?

- Sometimes the Christian church can seem like "a center for merchandise," just as the temple had become. In what ways have you seen this? How does this transform the church from a reflection of the heart of God and get in the way of sharing it?

CONSIDER THIS

Jesus is the One you've been waiting for your whole life! Consider the specific ways Jesus has come into the world for you and your life. In what ways does Jesus fulfill what you've been waiting for? End by praising Jesus for being the One you need—as the Light of Truth, the Lamb of God, the Mighty One, and the Living Expression of God!

Lesson 3

God Loves the World

JOHN 3:1–4:42

"For this is how much God loved the world—
he gave his one and only, unique Son as a gift.
So now everyone who believes in him will never perish
but experience everlasting life." (John 3:16)

One of the most memorable verses in the Bible has gotten more air-time than any other verse thanks to zealous sports fans who hold up large poster boards emblazoned with it. It also happens to be one of the most important verses in all of Scripture: John 3:16.

Read this verse, then read it again. Embedded within this revelation is the sweet, spectacular reality that sits at the heart of John's gospel and this lesson: God loves the world! Not only that, but we discover *how much* God loved the world: He loved the world so much that he gave the world a gift. But not just any gift. God gave us his Son, his "one and only, unique Son"—for you and your world. A prominent religious leader, Nicodemus, discovered this truth when he came to Jesus in secret. So did a woman from a hated ethnic group who had been married five times when Jesus publicly came into her life.

Regardless of who these people were or what they had done or not done, Jesus' message was simple: God loves the world. May this lesson touch you as much as it touched Nicodemus and the Samaritan woman.

Discover the Heart of God

- After reading John 3:1–4:42, what did you notice, perhaps for the first time? What questions do you have? What did you learn about the heart of God?

- How much did John say God loved the world? What does this say about the heart of God?

- What did John say happens to those who trust in the Son? What about those who don't?

- Why was the Samaritan woman surprised that Jesus asked her for a drink? How did Jesus respond to the woman's surprise? How did the woman respond when Jesus revealed that he was the Anointed One, and how did her response affect other people?

- When the disciples returned, how did they react when they discovered Jesus had been hanging out with the Samaritan woman? How did Jesus respond?

Explore the Heart of God

- What does it mean to be reborn from above? How does one act who is born from above?

- John said that Jesus was "the One who comes from above and is above everything and speaks of the highest realm of all!" (3:31) What did John mean by this, and how should this impact how we receive what Jesus said?

- Who were the Samaritans, and why were they so significant to the story? Why was it significant that Jesus asked a woman for a drink of water?

- What did Jesus mean by "living water"? What was the "thirst" he was referring to, and why won't people be thirsty again when they drink what he offers? How did the Samaritan woman's secret life relate to Jesus' invitation?

- What did Jesus mean that "God is a Spirit, and he longs to have sincere worshipers who worship and adore him in the realm of the Spirit and in truth" (4:24)?

- What did Jesus mean when he said, "My food is to be doing the will of him who sent me and bring it to completion" (4:34)?

Experience the Heart of God

- Jesus told Nicodemus that everyone must experience a rebirth in order to experience the eternal life of God's kingdom realm. Have you yourself experienced a rebirth? Describe that experience.

- How should John 3:16 impact every single person on the planet? How has it impacted you and your daily life?

- Jesus' interaction with the Samaritan woman teaches us a powerful lesson about befriending people who might be considered "unclean" or on the "outside." Who might those people be in your life, and how can you follow Jesus by doing what he did?

- Jesus said to the woman that anyone who drinks the living water he offers "will never thirst again and will be forever satisfied" (4:14). What "thirsts" do you have? How do you want Jesus to satisfy your life?

Share the Heart of God

- John's gospel tells us that God didn't send Jesus into the world to condemn it but to rescue it. Why is it important that this truth sits at the heart of our efforts at sharing the heart of God? How does it impact how we share God's heart?

- What should we learn from Jesus' interaction with the Samaritan woman at the well as we share the heart of God?

- The woman at the well will go down in history as the first New Testament evangelist to win a city to Christ. God is faithful to use anyone to reach others when we are honest to tell others that Jesus knows everything we've ever done and still loves us. What can we learn from this woman's story, and how God might want to use us?

- Who in your life do you think Jesus has prepared you to "harvest"? What stage of harvesting might you be working: planting, laboring, or harvesting?

CONSIDER THIS

John revealed how much God loves us: he gave his Son to the world as a gift, and everyone who trusts in him for their salvation will never die but experience eternal life. Close by praising God for this sweet reality: that God loved you so much he died for you, and that you will forever enjoy his eternal communion love because of your belief in his Son!

Lesson 4

The Wonder-Working Son

JOHN 4:43–5:47

*"I speak to you timeless truth. The Son is not able
to do anything from himself or through my own initiative.
I only do the works that I see the Father doing, for the Son
does the same works as his Father."* (John 5:19)

In the last lesson, we encountered the simple but spectacularly sweet revelation truth that God loves the world. He loved the world so much that he gave his Son, Jesus, to the world to rescue it. Now we begin to see the works and wonders of God's gift.

First we encounter a frantic Roman government official whose son was dying. He was so desperate for help that he traveled twenty miles to find Jesus and asked him to heal his son. The very hour he believed in his heart, his son's fever broke! Then, when Jesus returned to Jerusalem, he encountered another man in need: someone who had been disabled was lying at a pool for the sick. Jesus asked the man if he wanted to be healed; the man didn't know what hit him! For Jesus told him to pick up his mat and walk—and he did, for the first time in thirty-eight years.

These works and wonders continued from then on, because as Jesus said, "Every day my Father is at work, and I will be too!" (5:17). Discover the wonder-working Son and what he might have in store for you.

33

Discover the Heart of God

- After reading John 4:43–5:47, what did you notice, perhaps for the first time? What questions do you have? What did you learn about the heart of God?

- What happened in the lives of the government official from Capernaum and his household when Jesus healed his son?

- Compare the reaction of the Jewish leaders and Jesus to the crippled man.

- What does 5:17–32 say about Jesus' identity? List all the things we learn about him.

- Jesus talked about two kinds of people and their responses. Who are they, and what do they receive?

Explore the Heart of God

- What did Jesus mean that people "never believe unless you see signs and wonders" (4:48)? Why does this seem to be the case with people?

- What does the story about the government official in Capernaum tell us about the power of miracles and how God uses them to draw people to himself?

- Why were the Jewish leaders angry that the crippled man was carrying his mat? What does this say about them?

- Why was it significant that Jesus called God his "Father"? What does this say about his identity?

- How is it that Moses incriminated the Jewish leaders (5:45)?

Experience the Heart of God

- Describe a time when God did something extraordinary for you and it drew you closer to his heart.

- In this lesson, we see Jesus raise a boy back to life and heal a disabled man. What do you truly long to happen in your life to bring healing, release, and new life?

- Jesus said anyone who believes in him and his message has "passed from the realm of death into the realm of eternal life!" (5:24). Describe the moment when you yourself believed and passed over from death to new life.

Share the Heart of God

- There are countless people in our day who need to experience the heart of God through a healing touch and restoration. In what ways might you be able to bring such restoration to people in your life?

- In Jesus' day, the Jewish leaders had a hard time accepting who Jesus was. Why do you think people have a hard time accepting Jesus in our day?

- Jesus said that John the Immerser was a "blazing, burning torch" in his testimony about Jesus' person and identity. How might it look in your life to be such a witness for Jesus at your work or school, in your neighborhood and family?

CONSIDER THIS

The good-gift–giving God is always at work in people's lives, which we see on full display in the life of the Son of God, like in the life of the government official and the disabled man. Spend time asking God how you need him to work in your life. Then praise him for the Son who works wonders on your behalf!

Lesson 5

The Bread of Life and Living Water

JOHN 6:1–7:52

*"I, the Son of Man, am ready to give you
what matters most, for God the Father has
destined me for this purpose."* (John 6:27)

Jesus is more than enough for each of us. He is ready to give us what matters most, what fulfills us and fills us most.

We find two unique names of Jesus that point to this revelation truth: Jesus is the Bread of Life and the Living Water. As our Bread of Life, Jesus satisfies our hunger; as our Living Water, he quenches our thirst. When we find our satisfaction in Jesus, we won't be hungry for the stuff of this world; when we come to Jesus and drink what he offers, our innermost being will burst with what we need most. In other words, Jesus is more than enough for every single one of our needs!

May the meditations of our lesson and Scripture be the anthem of our life. May we find everything we long for in Jesus.

Discover the Heart of God

- After reading John 6:1–7:52, what did you notice, perhaps for the first time? What questions do you have? What did you learn about the heart of God?

- What was the reason Jesus gave that the people came looking for him? Why *didn't* they? What does this say about people's pursuit of Jesus and the heart of God?

- Why did so many people end up turning their backs on Jesus and refusing to be associated with him? Why didn't Peter and the twelve disciples themselves leave?

- How did Jesus respond when his brothers pushed him to publicly perform miracles in Judea rather than in the countryside?

- A controversy brewed among the people so that there was disagreement over his identity. List the various answers people gave for who Jesus was.

- Where did Jesus say he came from? And what was Jesus referring to when he said, "From where I am you cannot come" (7:34)?

Explore the Heart of God

- Why did the massive crowds continue following Jesus everywhere? What does this say about Jesus, who he was, and what people saw in him? What does it say about the crowds?

- The people came to Jesus for perishable food, but Jesus promised something better. What was it he promised, and why does what he gives satisfy us more than earthly "food"? What does it mean to "eat" Jesus' body? How about sharing his "food" with the world?

- What did Jesus mean when he said his words were "Spirit-breathed"? How are they "life-giving"?

- What do you think Jesus' brothers' motives were when they pushed him to perform his miracles publicly in Judea rather than in the countryside?

- How did the Old Testament prophecies about Jesus answer the crowds' questions about him? See Psalm 89:3–4, Micah 5:2, Matthew 1:1 and 2:1, and Luke 2:4.

- What did Jesus mean when he said, "All you thirsty ones, come to me! Come to me and drink! Believe in me, so that rivers of living water will burst out from within you; flowing from your innermost being, just like the Scripture says!"? What does this say about the heart of God?

Experience the Heart of God

- Jesus' question, "Where will we buy bread?" was a test for Philip to see if he would look to Jesus to supply all that was needed and not consider their limited resources. When was a time Jesus tested your trust in him to supply your needs? How did it turn out?

- Jesus said he was the Bread of Life. What "hunger" do you need to bring to Jesus to satisfy?

- Are you thirsty? How would it look in your own life to come to Jesus and drink what he offers? What do you need quenched by Jesus' rivers of living water?

Share the Heart of God

- Why do people nowadays turn their back on Jesus and refuse to be associated with him?

- How might it look to share the Bread of Life with those in your life?

- It seems clear the crowds were confused about Jesus' identity. What are some things people in our day are confused about regarding who Jesus is and what he came to do?

CONSIDER THIS

Jesus promises that rivers of Living Water will burst forth from him into our hearts when we come to him parched from life. He also promises to offer us his satisfaction as the Bread of Life when we come to him empty. Consider the areas of your life that need Christ's thirst-quenching water and hunger-satisfying bread, believing that all we have in him is more than enough.

Lesson 6

The Light to the World

JOHN 8:1–9:41

*"I am light to the world and those who embrace me
will experience life-giving light, and they will
never walk in darkness."* (John 8:12)

One of the most memorable Christian songs happens to have a re-markable story behind it. "Amazing Grace" was the result of the piercing light of Christ radically transforming the life of one "wretch," John Newton. In his own words, "I sinned with a high hand, and I made it my study to tempt and seduce others." Eventually, Newton became found, regained his sight, and was freed from a life of sin—all because of the Light of the World.

The same amazing grace that touched Newton's life is on full display in our lesson today. At every turn in John's gospel, the Light of the World offers life-giving light so people don't have to walk in darkness. An adulteress woman experienced his light, as did a man born blind. Though the religious leaders rejected his light, Jesus taught that when people embrace him, the light of truth will be released into their life. He also revealed that true freedom is found in him, the great I AM!

Jesus said his "light is the light that pierces the world's darkness" (9:5). Keep reading to experience the same light that Newton himself experienced!

Discover the Heart of God

- After reading John 8:1–9:41, what did you notice, perhaps for the first time? What questions do you have? What did you learn about the heart of God?

- Describe the two very different responses both the Pharisees and Jesus had toward the woman caught in adultery. Why did the Pharisees ultimately bring the adulterous woman to Jesus?

- How did the Pharisees respond to Jesus' testimony about himself? How did Jesus respond, and who did Jesus say confirmed his testimony?

- Why did Jesus say the Jewish leaders didn't understand his message? What did Jesus say the Jewish leaders would be doing if they truly knew God?

- When the disciples saw the blind man, they asked, "Teacher, whose sin caused this guy's blindness, his own, or the sin of his parents?" (9:2). How did Jesus respond? According to Jesus, why was he blind?

Explore the Heart of God

- What were the Pharisees' reasons for their harsh treatment of the adulterous woman? What does this say about the religious practices of the Pharisees?

- Instead of answering the Pharisees' questions about the adulterous woman, Jesus wrote in the dust with his finger. Some have suggested he was writing down the sins of all who were there. How does this deepen the meaning of his statement, "Let's have the man who has never had a sinful desire throw the first stone at her" (8:7)?

- What did Jesus mean that he was the "light to the world"? How does Jesus provide "life-giving light" so people never have to "walk in darkness" (8:12)?

- Jesus said, "I have existed before Abraham was, for I Am!" (8:58). What deeper reality was Jesus sharing about himself? Why did this enrage the Jewish leaders?

- Why do you think there was such division and disbelief among the Jewish leaders over Jesus healing the blind man? Why do you think the healed blind man threw himself at Jesus' feet, worshiped him, and believed in him?

- What did Jesus mean that he came to "judge those who think they see and make them blind," and "for those who are blind, I have come to make them see" (9:39)?

Experience the Heart of God

- How should Jesus' parting words to the woman at the well influence our own walk with Christ?

- In what ways has Jesus provided "life-giving light" for you and your life?

- Describe the moment you met Jesus. What happened to you? What did Jesus do for you?

- Jesus said in order for our sins to be removed, we need to acknowledge our blindness. Consider blind areas in your life you might need to confess to find forgiveness of your sins.

- "Amazing Grace" echoes the blind man's testimony: "All I know is that I was blind and now I can see for the first time in my life!" (9:25). Give thanks to God for the ways he has given you "sight" and healed your "blindness."

Share the Heart of God

- How should Jesus' handling of the woman caught in adultery guide how we share the heart of God by handling other people's sin?

- In John 8:12, Jesus described himself as the "light to the world" who helps people "experience life-giving light" so they "never walk in darkness." Remarkably, Jesus also described us as "lights," saying *our* lives "light up the world" (Matthew 5:14). How can you show and share Jesus in a way that helps people walk out of the darkness?

- Jesus declared that when people embrace the truth of his teachings, "it will release more freedom" into their lives (8:32). Who do you know who needs the freedom of Christ?

- In the story of the blind man, Jesus said his blindness happened to him so that people "could watch him experience God's miracle" (9:3). God had a purpose for his problems. How might this revelation be of comfort to those with whom you share the heart of God?

CONSIDER THIS

"Amazing grace how sweet the sound that saved a wretch like me; I once was lost but now am found, was blind but now I see."[1] Like the adulterous woman, we were all caught in our sin and deserving of punishment. Yet God had compassion on us, forgave us, and restored us. Praise him for this grace, and respond to Jesus' words: "Go, and from now on, be free from a life of sin" (8:11).

---

1 John Newton, "Amazing Grace," Public Domain.

Lesson 7

The Good Shepherd, Resurrection, and Life Eternal

JOHN 10:1-11:57

"I am the Resurrection, and I am Life Eternal.
Anyone who clings to me in faith, even though he dies,
will live forever. And the one who lives by believing in me
will never die. Do you believe this?" (John 11:25-26)

Our world is aching for *hope*, isn't it? Hope for a job or a better job, for safety, security, and health—hope for a better tomorrow. What is our Christian hope? The Bible says we can have ultimate hope now *and* later!

We're reminded of this with Lazarus' story in John's gospel. He was Jesus' friend and Miriam's[1] and Martha's brother, and he became sick. Because their hope was in Jesus, they asked him for help. Yet Jesus didn't come right away. When he finally did, it was too late; Lazarus had died. But Jesus did something remarkable: he raised Lazarus from the dead! He stepped into this hopeless situation and brought resurrection and new life. Because, you see, resurrection and new life is our ultimate hope—both now

---

1 "Miriam" is a literal rendering from the original Greek and Aramaic, which leave the Hebrew as is. She is more widely known as Mary, the sister of Martha.

and later. John's gospel says that's who Jesus is and what Jesus ultimately came to offer.

We are reminded today of the renewing, resurrecting life of Christ that's ours right now—as much as it is later. Discover afresh the Good Shepherd who's ready to work many miracles and acts of mercy in your life!

Discover the Heart of God

- After reading John 10:1–11:57, what did you notice, perhaps for the first time? What questions do you have? What did you learn about the heart of God?

- What does Jesus say is the one thing on the mind of the "thief"? What does Jesus say is his desire instead?

- The religious leaders asked for proof from Jesus that he was the Messiah. What "proof" did Jesus say he gave them? Why did he say they refuse to follow him despite that proof?

- Why did the religious leaders accuse Jesus of blasphemy? How did he respond?

- Why did Jesus say he waited to come to Lazarus' aid? What did Jesus say was the purpose behind Lazarus' death? How did the people respond when Jesus raised him from the dead? How about the Pharisees?

- What did Jesus promise people who cling to him in faith?

Explore the Heart of God

- What does Jesus' parable about the kind shepherd teach you about the heart of God?

- What does it mean that Jesus is the "Gate"? What does it tell you about Jesus that he is named the "Good Shepherd"?

- How did Miriam respond to Jesus' delay with Lazarus? How about Martha? What did their responses to his arrival reveal about their faith?

- What did Jesus mean when he said he was the "Resurrection" and "Life Eternal"?

- When Jesus finally arrived at Lazarus' tomb, he wept. What does this tell us about the heart of our Savior?

Experience the Heart of God

- List the ways Jesus cares for us as our Good Shepherd. How has he cared for you?

- Have you ever experienced a delay in answered prayer? What was that like, and what did you learn through it?

- How does it make you feel to know Jesus wept at the death of his friend, when he was confronted by the chaos and pain of life?

Share the Heart of God

- How might the fact that Jesus is a Good Shepherd be good news for your friends and family who don't yet know the heart of God?

- In 10:19–20, there was some confusion about Jesus' person and identity. How are people in our world and in your life similarly confused about who Jesus is?

- When Jesus arrived at his dead friend Lazarus' tomb, literally "his heart melted with compassion" for his friends and family. How might this picture be good news for people you know who experience hardship and pain?

CONSIDER THIS

We discover that not only is Jesus our Resurrection and Life, he is our Good Shepherd. He leads, guides, and cares for us according to his loving-kindness. Use the words of this trusted hymn to guide your closing prayer: "Savior, like a shepherd lead us, much we need Your tender care; In Your pleasant pastures feed us, for our use Your folds prepare."[2] Amen.

2   Dorothy A. Thrupp, "Savior, Like a Shepherd Lead Us," Public Domain.

Lesson 8

The Revelation of Christ's Purpose

JOHN 12:1–13:38

"Even though I am torn within, and my soul is in turmoil,
I will not ask the Father to rescue me from this hour of trial.
For I have come to fulfill my purpose—to offer myself to God.
So, Father, bring glory to your name!" (John 12:27–28)

Great people are defined by great purposes. Whether in business or politics, technology or humanitarian causes, or even everyday life, pick a person in these endeavors and you're sure to find them striving for a great purpose.

Jesus was such a person because he was defined by a great purpose—the greatest purpose ever! But what was it? Was it to show us how to live the best life possible? Or teach us how to love God and our neighbor? While these were part of his life, we discover his true purpose in this lesson.

That purpose was anticipated with a number of unusual events: Miriam anointed Jesus with a perfume often used in burial customs; Jesus talked about offering himself to God by being lifted off the ground—imagery that anticipated what was to come; he washed the feet of his disciples, like a humble servant purifying his followers; and he predicted disciples would betray and deny him unto death.

Great people are defined by great purposes. What was Jesus' purpose? To love the world by dying for it. He invites us to do likewise: to detach our lives from this world and love it with a cross-shaped love.

Discover the Heart of God

- After reading John 12:1–13:38, what did you notice, perhaps for the first time? What questions do you have? What did you learn about the heart of God?

- How did the disciples respond to the woman who anointed Jesus' feet? How did Jesus?

- How did the crowds react to Jesus' visit to Jerusalem? Why didn't the disciples fully understand the importance of what was taking place when Jesus arrived?

- Why did John say Jesus' critics still refused to believe in him, even after all the many signs? What did Jesus say would happen to those who hear his words and yet refuse to believe?

- What did Jesus do just before the evening meal before Passover? How did the disciples respond?

- What was the "new commandment" Jesus gave his disciples? What purpose does it serve?

Explore the Heart of God

- If Jesus had wanted to, he could have asked his Father to rescue him from death. Why didn't he? What does this say about the heart of God and Jesus' purpose?

- What do the prophecies from Isaiah in 12:38–39 tell us about Jesus' critics and unbelief?

- How did Jesus' washing of his disciples' feet represent and illustrate the full measure of his love for them?

- Jesus said, "Whoever receives the message I send receives me, and the one who receives me receives the Father who sent me" (13:20). What did he mean by this, and how does this look practically in people's lives? How does this insight impact our understanding of salvation and belief?

- How does God ultimately unveil the glory of the Son of Man?

- Why is Jesus' "new commandment" a *new* command? How is it different from the one he gave to love God and love people?

Experience the Heart of God

- How might you use things, whether money or otherwise, to serve Christ and his kingdom, just like Miriam did? How might you learn from Miriam in this part of your life?

- Are you sharing in God's heart by abandoning yourself fully to him and detaching your life from this world? Or do you tend to love your life and pamper yourself?

- John mentioned that certain Jewish leaders who believed in Jesus kept it a secret. Why do you think people nowadays keep their belief in Jesus a secret?

- Judas is often looked to as the ultimate betrayer. Yet people still follow in his footsteps. How might it look today to betray Jesus?

Share the Heart of God

- John said the eyewitnesses to Jesus' miracles kept spreading the news about him. What could you spread about Jesus' intervention and care for you to those in your life?

- How might it look practically to follow Jesus' example of washing people's feet in your own life by sharing the heart of God? List an example or two.

- How would it look practically to share the heart of God by loving people as Christ loved you?

CONSIDER THIS

In another letter, John said that we know what love is because Jesus Christ showed us by dying for us (1 John 3:16). Jesus loved with a cross-shaped love. His love was a love that served, which his basin-and-towel love illustrated. Close by asking Jesus to help you love your world with this same love.

Lesson 9

The Way to Life

JOHN 14:1–15:25

"I am the sprouting vine and you're my branches.
As you live in union with me as your source, fruitfulness will
stream from within you—but when you live separated
from me you are powerless." (John 15:5)

You don't have to be a botanist to know that when branches or stems of flowers are severed from their tree or flowering bush, it spells imminent death! The same is true for our life with God through Jesus.

We've been seeing throughout this study of John's gospel that God loves the world, and he offers everyone his new life. But there is only one way we can find and maintain that life: it's through Jesus. We see that Jesus is the Way to that life, the Truth of that life, and the very Definition of that Life. We also see that he is the *only* Way, Truth, and Definition, for no one comes to the Father except through union with Jesus. He's also the one who maintains our new life: as we live in union with Jesus, we will be fruitful; if we separate ourselves from Jesus, we will be powerless.

Jesus truly is the One "who birthed faith within us and who leads us forward into faith's perfection," as Hebrews 12:2 says. Find in Jesus the life you've always wanted; stay with Jesus to empower and maintain that life.

Discover the Heart of God

- After reading John 14:1–15:25, what did you notice, perhaps for the first time? What questions do you have? What did you learn about the heart of God?

- Jesus described himself as being like a vine. How did Jesus explain this important spiritual metaphor? What did he mean by it?

- What did Jesus say is the greatest love of all? How did he show us this kind of love? With what kind of love did Jesus say he loves us? How does this deepen your understanding of the heart of God?

- Why didn't Christ call his disciples servants? What did he call them, and us, instead? Why did he call us/them this?

- Who is the Divine Encourager? What is his purpose? List all the ways he acts in our lives. See 14:15–31, 15:26–27, and 16:5–16.

Explore the Heart of God

- What did Jesus mean that no one comes to God except through union with him?

- "To know me is to know my Father too," Jesus said (14:6). How is this true, that anyone who has seen or known Jesus has seen and known the Father?

- Who does Jesus say he sent to us? What does he do for us?

- Jesus said he left us the gift of his peace. What is this peace? How is it perfect?

- What does it mean to remain in life-union with Jesus? What happens if we don't?

Experience the Heart of God

- In what ways should Jesus' promise not to leave us helpless or abandon us comfort and reassure you?

- How would it look in your life to remain in life-union with Jesus? List some ways you can continue to share in the heart of Christ each and every day.

- How does it make you feel to know you are an intimate friend of Christ? How might this change your relationship with him if you truly viewed it that way?

Share the Heart of God

- How difficult is it in our day to share God's heart in such an exclusive way by suggesting access to it is through Jesus and Jesus alone? Is it possible to make it easier? Why or why not?

- Jesus said that people who follow him will do the same things he did—except in greater measure. Make a list of the ways you can share Christ's heart and in his works.

- Our lesson ends with a word of warning from Jesus: "Since they persecuted me, they will also persecute you" (15:20). Why should this encourage us as we share the heart of God and gospel of Christ?

CONSIDER THIS

The only way to the Father's life is through union with Jesus; the only way to maintain that life is through the power of Jesus. He is the true way to life; he is the true vine of life. Commit to finding the life of God through no other means than Jesus; commit to living in union with Jesus to maintain the life of God.

Lesson 10

Be Courageous. Jesus Has Conquered, and You Have Help!

JOHN 15:26–17:26

"Everything I've taught you is so that the peace which is in me will be in you and will give you great confidence as you rest in me. For in this unbelieving world you will experience trouble and sorrows, but you must be courageous, for I have conquered the world!" (John 16:33)

Have you ever realized how much courage it takes to live as a Christian? Maybe you've never thought of your journey with Christ in this world as a *courageous* one, but it is. Jesus says so!

In a world with loose ethics—financial, personal, sexual—we're called to live to a higher standard, which can often cost us. We believe in one God who sent his Son to die for the sins of the world and then was raised back from the dead—which sounds crazy to modern ears! We've been commissioned to invite people to change their lives and follow Jesus—and promised we'll be persecuted for it. So, yes, the Christian life takes courage!

But never fear: Jesus says we can have courage in this world because he has conquered it! He has also sent us a Divine Encourager who guides us into all truth and encourages us. While we may have troubles and sorrows in this life, we are not alone and not without power to live the life he's called us to live!

Discover the Heart of God

- After reading John 15:26–17:26, what did you notice, perhaps for the first time? What questions do you have? What did you learn about the heart of God?

- How did Jesus say the disciples' sadness would turn to joy after Christ's death? In what way did Jesus compare this to childbirth?

- Before Jesus' death, the disciples said they finally "understand" and "know." What was it they finally understood and acknowledged?

- What does chapter 17 further reveal about Jesus' identity and mission? Make a list.

- What did Jesus say eternal life means?

- List all the things Jesus prayed for in chapter 17.

Explore the Heart of God

- Who is the Divine Encourager, and why does he matter? What does he do for us?

- Why is it to our advantage that Jesus went away? Why is this reality important for our lives now?

- How should it impact our Christian life to know we will be persecuted and hated by the world because Christ was first hated and persecuted?

- What do some of Jesus' final words teach us about prayer?

- Jesus said that he has "conquered the world." What does he mean by this, and how should it encourage you?

Experience the Heart of God

- How should we respond to the knowledge that we will be hated and persecuted for Christ's sake?

- Is there anything right now "you've not been bold enough to ask the Father for" in Christ's name? Spend time in prayer now, being "sure you'll receive what you ask for" (16:24)!

- Not only did Jesus pray for his current disciples, he also prayed for his future ones—that's you! What do you resonate with the most from his prayer in 17:20–26?

Share the Heart of God

- In what way does the Divine Encourager work on behalf of people in your life who haven't yet trusted in Jesus? How should this guide our prayers that people would encounter the heart of God?

- Throughout John's gospel, he reiterated the truth that God sent Jesus to offer eternal life. In 17:3, he basically said eternal life means to experience and encounter the heart of God in Jesus. Who in your life needs such an experience and encounter?

- Before Jesus went to the cross, he prayed for his disciples. But not only for them, he also prayed for "all those who will one day believe in me through their message" (17:20). Spend time praying for those people in your life who you'd love to one day see believe in Christ.

CONSIDER THIS

Before Jesus went to the cross, he prayed for his current and future disciples. He asked his Father that he wouldn't take them and us out of the world, but that he would guard our hearts from the evil of this world and make us holy by his Word. May we take courage from this prayer—and from the conquering example of Christ and power of his Divine Encourager!

Lesson 11

It Is Finished, My Bride!

JOHN 18:1–19:42

When he had sipped the sour wine, he said,
"It is finished, my bride!" Then he bowed his head
and surrendered his spirit to God. (John 19:30)

Do you realize it is finished? Forever? Done with? Do believe deep down that there is no need to strive to make things right between you and God? That there is no more sacrifice needed for the sins of the world?

Up until around 33 AD, this idea was preposterous! Because sacrifices *were* needed, for every single person. Then another one after that, and then another. Every day, priests would continue the ritualistic practice of offering the same sacrifices again and again. This practice would have kept going on and on for millennia because, as Hebrews 10:1 says, those sacrifices couldn't ultimately take away sin's guilt. That all changed with Jesus! Because, as he announced from the cross with his last dying breath, "It is finished, my bride!"

Do you know what this means? This lesson reminds us that we don't have to try to earn God's favor or burn ourselves out trying to perfectly fulfill empty religious rituals or strive to get God to like us more than he *loved* us by enduring the full agony and weight of the cross! The reason why is because Jesus' death worked. His suffering death was the *final* sacrifice.

Discover the Heart of God

- After reading John 18:1–19:42, what did you notice, perhaps for the first time? What questions do you have? What did you learn about the heart of God?

- Where did Jesus say his authority came from when Pilate was interrogating him? Why did Jesus say he came into the world when Pilate asked if he was a king? What was Pilate's response?

- In his version of the Passion, John described the various punishments leading up to Jesus' death in 19:1–37. List these events, and then explain how this deepens your appreciation of the cross of Christ.

- What was Pilate's ultimate verdict? What was the Jewish leaders'?

- Throughout Jesus' capture, trial, crucifixion, and death, various Old Testament prophecies were fulfilled. List them from 19:1–19:37.

- Who helped bury Jesus? Why is one of these people significant?

Explore the Heart of God

- When the mob came for Jesus and Jesus told them who he was, they fell backward. What does this show about the final events of Christ's life leading to his death?

- At one point during his interrogation, Jesus answered, "You would have no power over me at all, unless it was given to you from above" (19:11). What does this prove about his death and his heart for people?

- Jesus, our Passover Lamb, was crucified at the very moment Jewish priests were slaughtering lambs in the temple. Because there were so many lambs to be killed, the priesthood in that day extended the time of slaughter from noon to twilight—the very hours Jesus was on the cross. How does this deepen the meaning of Christ's death?

- When Christ said, "It is finished," what did he mean? What was "finished"?

Experience the Heart of God

- How does it make you feel to know that Jesus didn't fight back and avoid suffering when he was arrested? What does this reveal about the heart of God for you?

- Has there ever been a time when you denied being a Christian or were embarrassed of your relationship with Jesus—like Peter? If so, what was that like?

- Given everything that Jesus endured through his punishment, what does the cross mean to you?

Share the Heart of God

- When Jesus was arrested, Peter struck the ear of the high priest's servant with his sword. This event is a vivid picture of how we can hinder people's ability to hear our message when we walk in angry offense toward others. In what ways could our own actions hinder our ability to share the heart of God?

- Pilate's question, "What is truth?" is a question people in our day ask, too—about a lot of things. What sorts of "truths" do people challenge? How can you share the heart of God in Jesus with them to answer those challenges?

- Before Jesus died he declared, "It is finished!" Why is this declaration such good news to those with whom you share the heart of God?

CONSIDER THIS

Jesus accomplished everything that was necessary for your salvation and being made right with God on that old rugged cross. As the old hymn reminds us, "For 'twas on that old cross Jesus suffered and died, to pardon and sanctify me."[1] Spend time thanking Jesus for everything he endured to pardon you once and for all—for all eternity.

---

1   George Bennard, "The Old Rugged Cross," Public Domain.

Lesson 12

An Empty Tomb, Lives Restored, and Mission Renewed

JOHN 20:1–21:25

Suddenly Jesus appeared among them and said, "Peace to you!"
Then he showed them the wounds of his hands and his side—
they were overjoyed to see the Lord with their own eyes! And he
told them, "Just as the Father has sent me, I'm now sending you."
(John 20:19–21)

Imagine launching a movement that threatened both the religious and political establishments. And then the leader of your movement was killed as an example for everyone else who might threaten those powers. How would you feel? What would you do next?

Now you know how the disciples would've felt in the days after Jesus' crucifixion! It's no surprise they gathered behind locked doors—they were terrified of payback from the Jewish and Roman leaders. It also makes sense many of them went back to their former professions as fishermen; what else were they going to do but what they knew best? And yet Jesus' movement wasn't finished because *he* wasn't finished!

Our journey through Jesus' fascinating story in John's gospel ends with an unexpected—yet predicted—twist: Jesus is alive! And when he revealed himself to his disciples, he sent them on mission to preach the forgiveness of sins. He even called Peter to follow him into his movement, restoring him to full fellowship after his betrayal.

John said all the world's books couldn't contain all of Jesus' wonders. May we add to those wonders by joining him in his mission of rescue and re-creation.

Discover the Heart of God

- After reading John 20:1–21:25, what did you notice, perhaps for the first time? What questions do you have? What did you learn about the heart of God?

- Who did Miriam think Jesus was when she encountered him in full, resurrected glory? What message did he give her to share with the disciples?

- What did Jesus tell the disciples when he visited with them concerning their commissioning and mission in the world?

- Why wasn't Thomas convinced Jesus was alive? What did he demand? How did Jesus respond?

- What was Peter's response when Jesus appeared on the shores of the Sea of Galilee? How did Jesus respond to Peter?

Explore the Heart of God

- What do various Old Testament prophecies say about Jesus' resurrection? See Psalm 2:6–8 and 16:10, Isaiah 53:10–12, Jonah 1:17, and Hosea 6:2.

- How do you suppose the Miriams and disciples felt when they found that Jesus' body was missing?

- Why is it significant for every believer that just as the Father sent Jesus, he has sent us?

- What do you think Jesus meant when he told Thomas, "There are those who have never seen me with their eyes but have believed in me with their hearts, and they will be blessed even more!" (20:29)?

- Why is it significant that the disciples went back to their old profession as fishermen?

- Why is it significant that Jesus asked Peter three times if he loved him? What does this say about God's heart of forgiveness?

Experience the Heart of God

- What does Jesus' actual, physical, bodily resurrection mean for you and your experience of the heart of God?

- Do you have doubts? If so, what are they? And how should Jesus' response to Thomas comfort you?

- Describe a time when you needed God's forgiveness. What was that like? How did you feel afterward?

Share the Heart of God

- How does it make you feel knowing God the Father has sent you on mission, just as he had sent his Son? What might he be sending you to do?

- Why do people doubt nowadays? What doubts do people have? What can we learn from Jesus' response when dealing with people in our own lives who doubt?

- John said that if all of Jesus' works were written down, there'd be no room in all the books of the world! The same is true of the mighty works he's done in our lives. What works has Jesus written in the book of your life that you can share as a testimony to the heart of God?

CONSIDER THIS

Peter proves that no matter how far we've fallen, God's restoration is right around the corner. He shows that God's forgiveness is wide and deep enough to cover a multitude of sins. Close by praying an ancient prayer of confession, seeking and savoring God's sweet restoration:

Most merciful God,
I confess that I have sinned against you
in thought, word, and deed,
by what I have done,
and by what I have left undone.
I have not loved you with my whole heart; I have not loved
    my neighbor as myself.
I am truly sorry and I humbly repent.
For the sake of your Son Jesus Christ,
have mercy on me and forgive me;
that I may delight in your will,
and walk in your ways,
to the glory of your name. Amen.

Encounter the Heart of God

The Passion Translation Bible is a new, heart-level translation that expresses God's fiery heart of love to this generation, using Hebrew, Greek, and Aramaic manuscripts and merging the emotion and life-changing truth of God's Word. If you are hungry for God and want to know him on a deeper level, The Passion Translation will help you encounter God's heart and discover what he has for your life.

The Passion Translation box set includes the following eight books:

Psalms: Poetry on Fire

Proverbs: Wisdom from Above

Song of Songs: Divine Romance

Matthew: Our Loving King

John: Eternal Love

Luke and Acts: To the Lovers of God

Hebrews and James: Faith Works

Letters from Heaven: From the Apostle Paul (Galatians, Ephesians, Philippians, Colossians, I & II Timothy)

Additional titles available include:

Mark: Miracles and Mercy
Romans: Grace and Glory
1 & 2 Corinthians: Love and Truth

THE
PASSION
TRANSLATION

thePassionTranslation.com